Deadliest Diseases
of All Time

HIV and AIDS

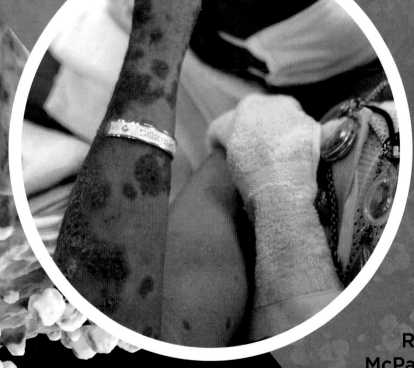

Randall
McPartland

Cavendish
Square

New York

Published in 2016 by Cavendish Square Publishing, LLC
243 5th Avenue, Suite 136, New York, NY 10016

CPSIA Compliance Information: Batch #WS15CSQ

All websites were available and accurate when this book was sent to press.

Library of Congress Cataloging-in-Publication Data

McPartland, Randall.
HIV and AIDS / Randall McPartland.
pages cm. — (Deadliest diseases of all time)
Includes index.
ISBN 978-1-50260-642-6 (hardcover) ISBN 978-1-50260-643-3 (ebook)
1. AIDS (Disease)—Juvenile literature. 2. HIV infections—Juvenile literature. I. Title.

RC606.65.C44 2016
616.97'92—dc23

2014046855

Editorial Director: David McNamara
Editor: Fletcher Doyle
Copy Editor: Cynthia Roby
Art Director: Jeffrey Talbot
Senior Designer: Amy Greenan
Senior Production Manager: Jennifer Ryder-Talbot
Production Editor: Renni Johnson
Photo Researcher: J8 Media

The photographs in this book are used by permission and through the courtesy of: Martinowi.cz/Shutterstock, cover
(background; used throughout book); PORNCHAI KITTIWONGSAKUL/AFP/Getty Images, cover (inset); MIKE NELSON/
AFP/Getty Images, 4; Dorling Kindersley/Getty Images, 7; Anup Shah/Getty Images, 8; File:Missionaries and steam train,
Congo, ca. 1900-1915 (IMP-CSCNWW33-OS10-83).jpg /Wikimedia Commons, 11; File:The National Archives UK - CO
1069-46-7.jpg /Wikimedia Commons, 13, iStockphoto.com/vidguten, 15; Holger Motzkau, Wikipedia/Wikimedia Commons,
16; Public Domain/File:Kaposi's sarcoma before.jpg/Wikimedia Commons, 18; ChaNaWit/Shutterstock, 20; Taro Yamasaki/The
LIFE Images Collection/Getty Images, 23; Dave Hogan/Hulton Archive/Getty Images, 28; File:RCGallo 9-08.JPG/Wikimedia
Commons, 32; National Institute of Allergy and Infectious Diseases (NIAID)/CDC, 35; Häggström, Mikael. "Medical gallery of
Mikael Häggström 2014/File:Symptoms of acute HIV infection.png/Wikimedia Commons, 36; ANNA ZIEMINSKI/AFP/Getty
Images, 42; ALEXANDER JOE/AFP/Getty Images, 45; Antonio Guillem/Shutterstock, 50; AP Photo/Eric Risberg, 54.

Printed in the United States of America

Contents

Introduction

S ociety's response to HIV/AIDS has changed since the 1980s, when panic, blame, and overreaction were common. The reason for the difference is the progress that has been made in treating the disease. New drugs can stop its development in the human body for years. However, did you know that after diseases of the heart and lungs, HIV/AIDS is the leading cause of death in the world? Or that 26 percent of all new HIV infections in the United States happen in the 13–24 age group?

It was shocking when basketball star Magic Johnson was diagnosed HIV positive in 1991. HIV, which is **Human Immunodeficiency Virus**, is the **virus** that causes AIDS. Johnson, who married his wife, Cookie, that year, immediately retired from the National Basketball Association (NBA). He returned the next year to play in the All-Star Game and also represented the United States in the Olympics.

There were many people who did not want him to return to basketball. There was fear he could infect others on the court. In 1992, the NBA issued guidelines for team doctors and trainers. Games could

Earvin "Magic" Johnson's announcement that he had contracted HIV and that he was retiring from the NBA sent out shock waves.

be stopped if someone suffered a cut, and players were removed if there was blood on their uniforms. People treating players were instructed to wear rubber gloves.

Much has changed since then. Johnson is a successful businessman and an owner of Major League Baseball's Los Angeles Dodgers. It is clear that being infected with HIV is no longer a death sentence. Unfortunately, this has led to many people letting down their guard and becoming complacent. HIV is like other viruses that cause illness, such as a flu virus, except that the human body can never rid itself of it. Once you contract the disease, you have it for life. And the illness it causes, AIDS, is deadly.

AIDS stands for **Acquired Immunodeficiency Syndrome**. When something is acquired, it means a person got it from somewhere else. Immunodeficiency means something is not working well in our **immune system**, which is our defense against getting sick. Syndrome means that there are symptoms, or signs of an illness.

The AIDS virus is a **germ**. There are five main types of germs: bacteria, fungi, parasites, protozoa, and viruses. A germ is a microorganism, or a very small living thing, that can cause disease in another living organism. It needs a cell to live in that will protect it and allow it to multiply. Once inside of a cell, the virus becomes active, and turns the cell into a virus-making machine.

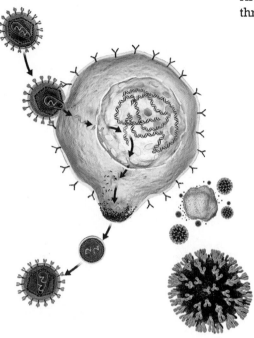

HIV infects human cells through receptors.

The human immunodeficiency virus can live for a long time in a body before any symptoms are seen. It attacks the **T cells** or CD4 cells, which are an important part of your immune system. When the immune system is weakened, infections that are usually mild can become serious. No matter how strong a person's immune system is to begin with, HIV may eventually weaken it so much so that the body can no longer defend itself from disease and even early death.

Science is just learning how the disease started, and how it spread.

Out of Africa: The Origin of AIDS

The origin of the Human Immunodeficiency Virus has been a subject of study and speculation for decades. Theories have been proposed and rejected. Through much research, scientists have pieced together the evidence and traced the start of the disease to monkeys in West Africa.

These monkeys—red-capped mangabeys and mustached guenons—are hunted by chimpanzees. Different viruses were passed from those monkeys to the chimpanzees that ate them. Those viruses combined to form simian immunodeficiency virus (SIV) in the chimpanzees.

One chimpanzee subspecies (a subdivision of a species) carried the disease that became AIDS. The subdivision lives only in the region between the Sanaga and Congo rivers. Scientists can isolate this subdivision because chimpanzees do not swim or migrate across rivers.

Chimpanzees were a primary part of the food chain along which HIV was passed into humans.

Humans in Western Africa picked up SIV from eating chimpanzee meat or coming into contact with the animal's tainted blood around 1921. These humans were mostly hunters. Many were infected this way, and they were infected with different types of HIV viruses. Among them were the HIV-1 and HIV-2 types.

One Source for Disease

There are different genetic groups of HIV. HIV-1 contains four genetic groups, including M and O. *National Geographic*, in 2014, published findings that group O and HIV-2 have remained in Central and Western Africa, and other strains have died out. However, group M grew and is the cause of 90 percent of AIDS cases around the world.

Two primary ways that HIV is spread are through sexual contact and blood **transmission**. Dr. Jacques Pépin, author of *The Origins of AIDS*, cited studies of heroin addicts that showed HIV was spread ten times faster by blood transmission than by sexual contact.

Oliver Pybus is an evolutionary biologist and infectious disease specialist at the University of Oxford. During an interview with *National Geographic*, Pybus said, "How the [HIV] virus first got from other species into humans has been studied in great detail. The question is: Why did one strain become a pandemic while others stayed local?"

The answer is that the virus had help from humans. The number of men who could have acquired group M

A train that ran from the Cape in South Africa to Cairo in Egypt stops in the Congo in the early years of the twentieth century. Missionaries are dressed in white.

by eating this subspecies of chimpanzee is about three. They started spreading the disease in Kinshasa, in what is now the Republic of the Congo. Viruses such as HIV need what is called an accelerator to spread. The first accelerator was the colonial transportation system built by Belgium and France. The virus was carried by the mostly male wage laborers who came into contact with female sex workers. Many of these workers were treated for sexually transmitted diseases with unsterilized needles in health clinics.

Unclean Conditions

These health clinics were the second accelerator. Dr. Pépin admitted that he might have infected some people because when he worked in the Congo he wasn't always diligent about checking how glass syringes were sterilized. These clinics treated many people as colonial doctors battled many diseases through the injection of **vaccines**.

The first blood sample that tested positive for HIV was found in 1959 in the twin cities of Leopoldville and Brazzaville. Leopoldville is now Kinshasa.

In 1960, the region was facing a crisis. Independence was gained from Belgium, whose white settlers fled. The economy failed and poverty greatly increased. The colonists had not educated the native population, so the United Nations sought teachers and bureaucrats who could help revive the country.

Haiti sent thousands of educated French-speaking workers to the Congo to help. However, poor women in the Congo turned to prostitution, and this accelerated the spread of HIV infections. When infected laborers reached ports at the mouth of the Congo River, the virus was exported.

Scientists believe one of the Haitian workers returned home infected with HIV in 1966. In Haiti, HIV needed another accelerator. Dr. Pépin stated that the disease was spread by an unsanitary **plasma** center. Plasma is the watery part of blood that carries blood cells. Plasma centers take donated blood and remove the red cells, then returned the red cell-depleted blood to the donor. The disease can be spread if new tubing isn't used

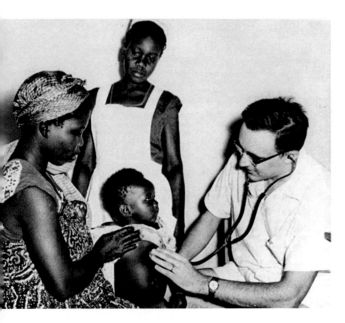

A British doctor treats a child at a clinic in 1957. Sterile procedures weren't always followed.

for each donor. The plasma center in Haiti sold 1,600 gallons of plasma to the United States each month.

Tourists who visited Haiti also brought the virus back to the United States.

HIV/AIDS Hit the US Hard

The United States has been hit a lot harder by the HIV/AIDS virus than has Europe. Here are three possible explanations:

- HIV, the virus that causes AIDS, arrived earlier in the United States, when little was known about the disease at that time.

- Epidemiologists believe that high-risk populations were concentrated in certain cities in the United States, particularly San Francisco. This helped the disease spread quickly among those populations.

- Americans also had a higher incidence of high-risk behavior, especially intravenous drug use, than Europeans, even before HIV arrived. The virus spreads most easily right after infection, so people who don't know they are infected and are sharing needles for intravenous drug use can pass HIV around quickly. In 1984, the rate of HIV infection among intravenous drug users was 50 percent in New York City and Edinburgh, Scotland, and 30 percent in Amsterdam, the Netherlands. In Europe, the governments responded quickly with needle exchange programs and free syringe distribution so drug users were not sharing needles. It took the United States a lot longer to begin exchange programs. With more intravenous drug users overall and more of those users sharing needles, the United States suffered from a higher infection rate than Europe did.

AIDS education improved on both continents, but death rates still climbed through the mid-1990s. In the United States, about nineteen people per one hundred thousand died of AIDS in 1995; in Great Britain and Europe, the number was three per one hundred thousand.

In Africa, there are much higher rates of infection than in the rest of the world. The primary cause of

Needles should never be left out for others to use. This is a common cause of the spread of HIV.

infection there is sexual contact between men and women. This has been explained by cultural difference. In some African countries, it is common for people to carry on several long-term heterosexual relationships at the same time. It can take a long time for an infected heterosexual partner to pass on HIV, but the chances of passing it on are higher right after infection. So when one of the partners becomes infected, all the members of a sexual network are at risk of getting the disease quickly.

The World Health Organization (WHO) reported that thirty-six million people have died since the first cases of AIDS were reported in 1981; 1.2 million of them died in 2012 alone. This makes AIDS the world's worst killer among infectious and deadly diseases.

A Closer History

1981 The CDC publishes a report of young gay men dying from infections because their immune systems aren't working. By the end of the year, 270 cases of severe immune deficiency and 121 deaths are reported.

1982–1983 The spread of HIV to heterosexual people in Africa is confirmed.

Luc Montagnier won the Nobel Prize for his discovery of the human immunodeficiency virus.

Luc Montagnier and Francoise Barre-Sinoussi discover a virus that is linked to AIDS.

1985 Ryan White is barred from a Kokomo, Indiana, middle school because he is diagnosed with AIDS.

1986 The virus that causes AIDS is named Human Immunodefiency Virus, or HIV.

1987 The US Food and Drug Administration (FDA) approves AZT, the first antiretroviral drug for fighting AIDS.

1990 On April 8, Ryan White dies at the age of eighteen in Riley Hospital for Children.

Congress approves the Ryan White Comprehensive AIDS Resources Emergency (CARE) Act to provide funds for treatment services and community-based care.

1995 The FDA approves the first **protease inhibitor**. These keep the AIDS virus from multiplying. This ushers in highly active antiretroviral therapy (HAART). By the next year, AIDS deaths in the United States decline by 40 percent.

2003 President George W. Bush announces a $15 billion President's Emergency Plan for AIDS Relief. This effort provides funds for HIV/AIDS treatment to fifteen nations.

2011 The National Institutes of Health reports that taking antiretroviral drugs at the onset of HIV leads to a dramatic reduction in HIV transmission to an uninfected heterosexual partner.

2012 Truvada becomes the first drug to be approved by the FDA specifically for use in the prevention of HIV transmission.

2014 Dr. Joep Lange, an AIDS researcher, dies when Malaysia Airlines Flight 17 is shot down over Ukraine.

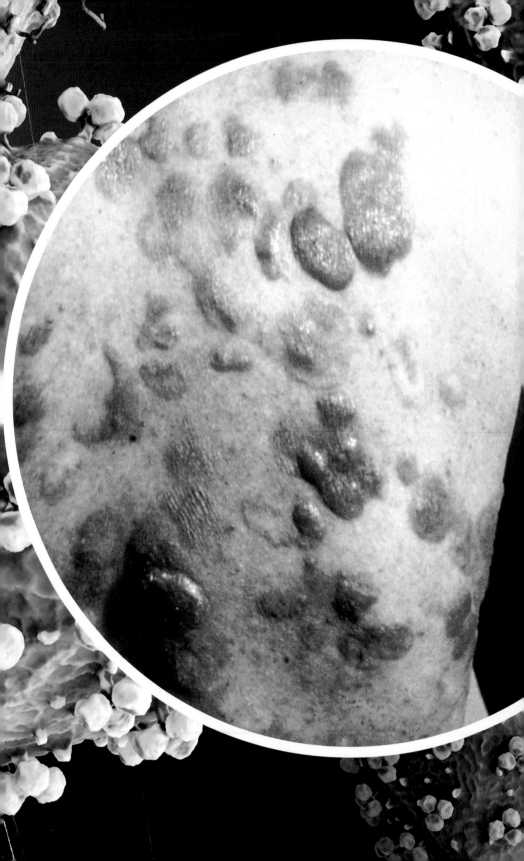

Giving HIV a Name

Acquired Immunodeficiency Syndrome does not have a long history, but it started much earlier than the 1980s, when it was discovered in the United States.

A French military doctor was alarmed by the rising death rate among workers building the Congo-Oceanic Railway in the 1930s. After performing autopsies, he found symptoms in twenty-six of the men that are found in AIDS patients. Those symptoms included atrophied brains and swollen bowel **lymph nodes**.

Frozen tissue samples, taken in 1969 from an African-American teenager who died in St. Louis, have been tested for the presence of HIV. The samples were tested because the teenager had died from AIDS-like symptoms. The HIV virus or a very close relative of the virus was found in the tissues.

Doctors received an early clue about the start of the AIDS epidemic when Kaposi's sarcoma afflicted an unusually large group of men.

The findings indicate that a type of HIV was present in the United States before the 1970s.

In 1981, the Centers for Disease Control and Prevention published a report on a rare lung infection called Pneumocystis carinii pneumonia (PCP). Five young men in Los Angeles, although previously healthy, had this infection and other unusual infections. This showed that their immune systems were not working. When news outlets published stories on the report, other doctors called the CDC to tell them about patients with similar infections.

Rare Cancer Found

The CDC also received information about otherwise healthy men developing a rare but aggressive cancer, **Kaposi's sarcoma**, in New York and San Francisco. The *New York Times* published a story on forty-one men afflicted with the cancer in those cities. By the end of that year, 270 men were found to have severe immune deficiency.

Before the 1980s, AIDS did not have a name or a known cause, but it was occurring. Due to the fact that it was diagnosed almost exclusively in gay men in 1981, the disease was called GRID (Gay-Related Immune Deficiency). In 1982, GRID was also found in people with **hemophilia**, or people whose blood does not clot. People with this condition are called hemophiliacs. They receive donated blood in the event that they are

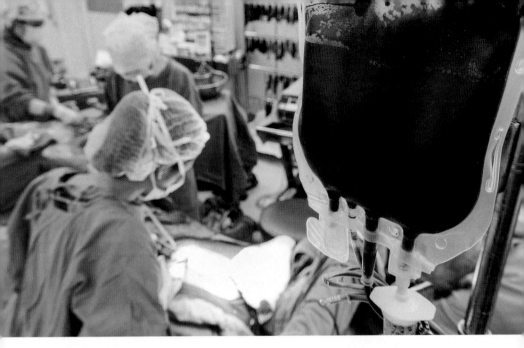

Infected blood used for transfusions during surgery spread HIV to infants, hemophiliacs, and the general population.

injured. The disease was also found in infants who had received blood transfusions. The CDC linked the disease to blood and acknowledged that there might be a problem with the blood supply. GRID-infected hemophiliacs had received contaminated blood, which caused their illness. Because it was now proven that the illness was not exclusive to the gay community, the name was changed from GRID to AIDS.

From there, the scope of the pandemic widened. In 1983, it became known that heterosexuals—who had not received donated blood—were developing AIDS. Two women were diagnosed with the disease after being infected by their male partners.

Fighting Fear

Ryan White, in 1985, was one of the first children to be diagnosed with AIDS. He was thirteen. Ryan was a hemophiliac who was exposed to the virus through a blood transfusion. When people in his town of Kokomo, Indiana, learned of his illness, he was banned from attending his middle school.

Ryan and his mother battled in court for his right to attend school. After they won their case, he was subjected to bullying. His family's house and car were vandalized. The family moved to another town, Cicero, Indiana, and life there was better for Ryan. He made new friends, got a job in a skateboard shop, and attended his senior prom. However, his health began to worsen halfway through his senior year. He died in April 1990 at the age of eighteen.

Brad Letsinger, who was one of Ryan's best friends, told the *New York Times*, "When he first came, a lot of people were really scared. But Ryan helped all of us to understand. He didn't want people to feel sorry for him. He hated that. He just wanted to be a regular kid."

It was hard for Ryan to be just a regular kid. He drew attention from around the world. Singer Michael Jackson bought him a car. Another singer, Elton John, was with him when he died, alongside Ryan's mother and grandparents. He

Ryan White battled to be treated as "just another kid" at school.

received phone calls from Vice President Dan Quayle, an Indiana native, and Senator Edward Kennedy of Massachusetts. President George H. W. Bush planted a tree in Indiana in Ryan's honor.

People said that Ryan's fight reduced bigotry around the country. The publicity helped pierce myths about AIDS, helping health experts and educators emphasize that the disease is not transmitted by casual contact and that it affects people from many walks of life.

The story of Ryan White moved the US Congress to enact the Ryan White Comprehensive AIDS Resources Emergency Act in 1990. The vote in the Senate was 95-4. It is the largest program designed only for people with HIV in the country. The Health Resources and Service Administration estimates that half a million people receive some help from this program every year.

Many Partners

In 1984, a man named Gaetan Dugas died from AIDS. He was not the first person to become infected, and did not bring the disease to the United States. Yet he was blamed for the spread of AIDS in the gay community. This was an incorrect assumption that stemmed from fear of the disease.

Dugas was a flight attendant based in New York. During a 1982 interview with the CDC, Dugas disclosed the fact that he engaged in a very high number of sexual encounters over several years—and he never used protection. A large number of AIDS patients over the following years were linked to Dugas. They either had unprotected sex with Dugas, or one of his past partners.

Dugas's story was used to shed light on the suffering in the gay community. This may have caused people to call AIDS "the gay disease." They were wrong. Fear of AIDS created a backlash against people. In New York in 1983, a doctor was told he would have to find another office if he continued to treat AIDS patients.

Spotlight on AIDS

Some bias against people with HIV stopped after the first celebrity's death from AIDS complications. Rock Hudson stood among Hollywood's most famous leading men. He was married to aspiring actress Phyllis Gates from 1955 to 1959. Hudson played opposite

Doris Day in the movie *Pillow Talk* in 1959, the first of a string of roles in which he held a romantic lead.

Hudson went to see a doctor in 1984 about a **lesion** on his neck, and it turned out to be Kaposi's sarcoma. One June 5, 1984, he was diagnosed with AIDS. He soon disclosed both his illness and his sexual orientation. Hudson died July 25, 1985, at the age of fifty-nine.

Among his friends was Elizabeth Taylor, one of the most accomplished female film actors ever. After Hudson died, Taylor became an AIDS activist. She helped to start the American Foundation for AIDS Research, and raised money for the organization.

One of the most celebrated early victims of AIDS in the United States was tennis player Arthur Ashe. He is still the only African-American male to win the US Open, which he did in 1968. He was also the first African American to be recruited to play in the Davis Cup (1963), to win the Australian Open (1970), to win Wimbledon (1975, over Jimmy Connors), and to be ranked number one in the world (1975).

Ashe retired from tennis in 1979 after suffering a heart attack. He underwent a quadruple bypass that year and a double bypass in 1983. He had emergency brain surgery in 1988, and a biopsy taken while he was in the hospital showed he had AIDS. Ashe had contracted the disease from an infected blood transfusion during his 1983 operation.

Ashe died from AIDS-related pneumonia on February 6, 1993. He left behind a wife and a daughter.

The United States Tennis Association opened Arthur Ashe Stadium in New York City's borough of Queens. The stadium today is the primary venue of the US Open.

How HIV Spreads

Scientists have researched how HIV is transmitted or spread. We know that HIV can infect anyone and be spread to anyone. We also know that HIV is passed from an infected person to an uninfected person through certain body fluids.

HIV can be spread through sexual contact between people of either gender in any combination. The body fluids that are infected with and can spread HIV are:

- Blood
- Semen and pre-seminal fluid (fluid that is released prior to semen)
- Vaginal secretions and menstrual blood
- Breast milk

The ways a person comes into contact with HIV-infected body fluids are:

- Unprotected sexual contact
- Sharing hypodermic needles
- Sharing needles used for tattoos or piercings
- Pregnancy, birth, and breastfeeding

Unprotected sexual contact means that a condom is not used. Sexual contact includes anything relating to the anus, vagina, penis, or mouth. The more sexual partners that a person has, the higher the chances of encountering someone who is infected with HIV. Many people continue to have unprotected sex, not knowing that they have HIV.

Sharing needles with an HIV infected person to inject substances such as heroin or steroids, even once, is enough of an opportunity for HIV to travel from one person to the next. This happens because blood from an HIV-infected person can stay in the needle, which is then injected into the next person.

Tattoos and piercings also use needles. Tattoo and piercing needles can become contaminated with HIV if they were used on an infected person. HIV can be removed from tattoo and piercing needles if they are sterilized, or cleansed so thoroughly that all germs are removed.

An infected woman can give HIV to her baby during pregnancy, at birth, and through breastfeeding. Breast milk doesn't contain as much HIV as blood, semen, or vaginal excretions, but even small amounts of HIV are enough to give a baby the virus.

AIDS: Fact or Myth

When a disease occurs, there are pieces of information or issues about it that are proven by science to be true, but there are also issues that take time to study and prove. While waiting for absolute answers to unproven issues, people can get confused. Here are some things we know.

Celebrity AIDS Deaths

Since the AIDS epidemic began, more than thirty-five million people have lost their lives to AIDS and AIDS-related illnesses. Here is a list of well-known people who have died from AIDS and AIDS-related illnesses.

1985 Rock Hudson, a legendary film star

1987 Michael Bennett, Broadway director of *Chorus Line*; Liberace, musician and entertainer

AIDS silenced the voice of Freddie Mercury in 1991.

1989 Amanda Blake, actor who played Miss Kitty on *Gunsmoke*; Robert Mappelthorpe, controversial photographer

1990 Halston, world-renowned fashion designer; Ryan White, teenage AIDS activist who fought to attend public school

1991 Freddie Mercury, musician and singer from the band Queen

1992 Robert Reed, the actor who played Mike Brady on *The Brady Bunch*; Isaac Asimov, science fiction writer; Anthony Perkins, actor

1993 Arthur Ashe, top-ranked tennis player; Rudolf Nureyev, world-renowned ballet dancer

1994 John Curry, Olympic figure skater; Elizabeth Glaser, activist for Pediatric AIDS, or AIDS relating to children; Dack Rambo, actor who played Jack Ewing on *Dallas*; Randy Shilts, author of the AIDS semi-fictional story *And the Band Played On*

1995 Paul Monette, writer, poet, and AIDS activist; Eric "Easy-E" Wright, rap musician

2000 Ofra Haza, popular singer

2003 Michael Jeter, Tony-winning actor; Gene Anthony Ray, American actor and dancer who starred in *Fame*

2005 Tori Dent, American poet

2006 Willi Ninja, dancer and choreographer

2007 James K. Lyons, American actor, film editor

2013 Sean Sasser, celebrity pastry chef and reality TV personality

These body fluids do not transmit HIV:
- Tears
- Saliva or spit
- Sweat
- Urine
- Feces

These activities will not pass along HIV, even if you do them with an HIV-infected person:

- Shaking or holding hands
- Hugging
- Coughing
- Sneezing
- Closed mouth, or social kissing
- Using the same swimming pools
- Using the same toilet
- Using the same household objects such as eating utensils

Giving Blood

Giving blood is an important and safe activity. When you give blood, your blood will be given to people who have been injured or to those undergoing surgery. You cannot get AIDS by giving blood to a blood bank or hospital.

In the years before 1985, there were some cases of people who developed HIV after receiving someone else's donated blood. Today, blood donors are carefully screened, and the donated blood is laboratory tested, thus transmission of HIV through donated blood is extremely rare.

Insect Bites

HIV cannot be transmitted or spread by insect bites, such as those by mosquitoes or bedbugs. HIV cannot reproduce or survive inside of these insects. A bug that has bitten a person will digest the blood meal before moving on to another human.

Prolonged Kissing

Researchers have located HIV in the saliva of infected people, but saliva contains substances that stop HIV from being infectious, meaning able to infect. Caution should be taken if either partner has sores or wounds in or around the mouth where infectious body fluids, such as blood, could enter in the case of open-mouth kissing.

Visits to the Doctor or Dentist

The chances of getting AIDS by visiting your doctor or dentist's office are extremely small. When your doctor or dentist treats a patient with AIDS, special precautions are taken before, during, and after the infected patient's treatment. Most health care providers follow strict infection control procedures that protect both patients and their health care providers from transmitting HIV and other viruses.

three Race for a Cure

T he alarming speed of the spread of HIV attracted worldwide attention. From 1981 to 1983, AIDS diagnosis and deaths had more than doubled. This pushed scientists to search even harder for solutions. The first step in finding a cure when a new disease strikes is to determine what causes the disease. The race for the discovery of the cause of AIDS created conflict between two countries and two of their best researchers.

In May of 1983, a virologist—a person who studies viruses—named Luc Montagnier claimed that he had found a virus that was linked to AIDS. He and his team from the Pasteur Institute in France had found a virus in the swollen lymph nodes of a patient. Montagnier named the virus LAV, which is a term for Lymphadenopathy Associated Virus. **Lymphadenopathy**, or a disease affecting the lymph nodes, is one of the first symptoms found in HIV

Dr. Robert Gallo, shown in 2008, was a pioneer in AIDS research.

patients who are progressing toward the development of full-blown AIDS.

The Pasteur Institute sent a sample of the virus to the Centers for Disease Control. In April of 1984, the United States Government held a press conference during which the secretary of health claimed that Robert Gallo of the National Cancer Institute had isolated a virus that caused AIDS—its name was HTLV-III. The official statement of the discovered virus was also followed by the announcement that Gallo had invented an accurate blood test that would detect HIV antibodies.

Sharing Credit

After the Food and Drug Administration approved Gallo's test, commercial kits for the **antibody** HIV test were licensed. The first time that the term HIV was used to describe the virus that caused AIDS was in 1986. It was determined that Gallo's HTLV-III and Montagnier's LAV were the same virus. An international committee ruled that both names should be replaced with HIV, or Human Immunodeficiency Virus. Eventually, Gallo and Montagnier shared credit for the discovery.

Some people blamed a lack of coordination between scientists in the United States and France for delaying HIV research. Others blamed the slow-moving government and a drug producer that refused to submit its drug for testing. Regardless, drug trials fell behind schedule. This caused anxiety among people with AIDS in the mid-1980s.

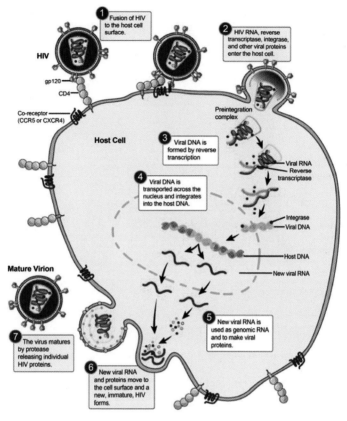

The seven steps of HIV cell infection and replication.

HIV on the Attack

Researchers seeking a cure for AIDS discovered why patients were getting sick. They found that HIV attacks and weakens a person's immune system, which is made up of cells that protect the body against harmful germs.

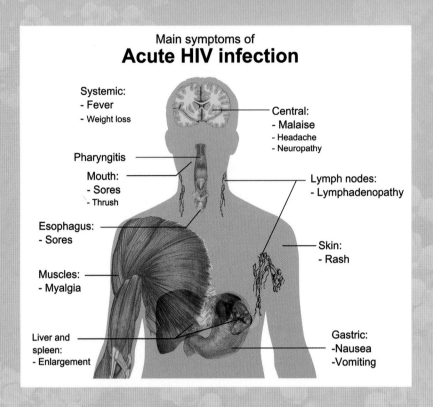

Main symptoms of
Acute HIV infection

Systemic:
- Fever
- Weight loss

Central:
- Malaise
- Headache
- Neuropathy

Pharyngitis

Mouth:
- Sores
- Thrush

Lymph nodes:
- Lymphadenopathy

Esophagus:
- Sores

Skin:
- Rash

Muscles:
- Myalgia

Liver and
spleen:
- Enlargement

Gastric:
-Nausea
-Vomiting

Warning Signs

Even though an infected person can live for years
without developing symptoms of HIV, there are some
common warning signs of HIV infection that may occur.
Even if you suffer from one or more of the common
warning signs, it does not mean that you have HIV. Many
other illnesses have the same symptoms. Only a
physician can diagnose an illness.

One of the first warnings HIV infected
people experience is swelling of the
lymph nodes. Lymph nodes are small,

bean-shaped organs that are part of the immune system. Lymph nodes are located inside of the body, but there are also lymph nodes that you can feel just under the skin. The nodes that you can feel are in the neck, armpits, and groin area. Lymph nodes store the army of immune cells, which trap and destroy invaders. A lymph node swells as the army of immune cells attacks the invaders that are trapped inside of it.

Other possible warning signs of HIV infection include:

- Frequent fevers
- Rapid weight loss
- Unexplained fatigue
- Breathing difficulties
- Excessive sweating
- Diarrhea that lasts longer than a week
- White spots or soars in the mouth and throat
- Pneumonia
- Memory loss
- Vision problems
- Depression
- Red, pink, purple, or brown blotches on or under the skin

Some of the most important cells of the immune system are:

- Helper T cells, or T4 cells, are cells that take part in immune system responses by recognizing targeted or unwanted cells and sending signals that activate killer T Cells. Their job is to scan the body for invaders. When an invader is encountered, they send out chemical signals that alert and activate the rest of the immune system.

- **B cells** are **white blood cells** that make antibodies. They are also called leukocytes, and they make up only 1 percent of your blood. Antibodies are proteins that the B cells create to destroy invaders. The proteins are specially made for each kind of invader. Antibodies produced by the body to fight HIV are called HIV antibodies. Other parts of your blood are red blood cells, platelets, and plasma.

- Killer T cells, or T8 cells, are cells that target and destroy other cells only when activated by helper T Cells. Killer T cells will attach themselves to cells that are abnormal, meaning infected with an invader. They will release chemicals to destroy the infected or abnormal cell.

When HIV attacks, the entire immune system is affected. HIV targets helper **T cells** and damages them. Damage to a helper T cell prevents it from doing the job of alerting the rest of the immune system. Communication between the helper cells and the other cells is cut off. Although HIV does not attack B cells directly, B cells may eventually lose their ability to function properly. Killer T cells also do not function properly, losing the ability to attack HIV-infected cells. HIV can be attacking the immune system cells for months or years without a person knowing it.

When HIV infects the immune system, it is weakened. A weakened immune system means that normally mild infections in the body can become serious or even deadly.

HIV Treatment

The first breakthrough in the treatment of AIDS patients came when the Food and Drug Administration approved the first anti-HIV drug, AZT, in 1987. AZT is an antiretroviral, meaning it targets retroviruses, such as HIV.

This drug could reduce the replication of the virus and slow its growth. Initially, it extended the life expectancy of AIDs patients by one year. However, it does not stop the disease. There were two other problems. First, the drug was very expensive, costing about $12,000 per year. After many protests by AIDS activists, the price, in 1989, was lowered by 20 percent. Second, HIV is able to mutate and become immune to the drug. Other drugs were needed, and some were soon approved.

FDA-approved drugs work to interrupt the process of HIV replication, but each type of drug does this in a different way. The types of approved anti-HIV drugs are:

- Protease Inhibitors—Drugs of this type work to interrupt HIV virus replication, and may keep HIV replication controllable for long periods of time.

- Nucleoside Reverse Transcriptase Inhibitors (NRTIs)—These drugs also interrupt HIV virus replication and may delay the appearance of opportunistic infections in persons with advanced HIV. These normally minor infections seize the opportunity presented by a weakened immune system to attack and sicken people severely.

- Non-Nucleoside Reverse Transcriptase Inhibitors, or NNRTIs—Drugs of this type interrupt HIV virus replication, but they do not slow the spread of HIV from cell to cell.

At the 1996 Vancouver International Conference on AIDS, Dr. David Ho of the Aaron Diamond AIDS Research Center announced that the use of three anti-retroviral drugs could all but halt the advancement of the disease. Dr. Ho's combination drug therapy is called highly active antiretroviral therapy or HAART.

Reducing Deaths

Ho also said therapy might rid the body of the disease in eighteen to thirty-six months, and was named *Time* magazine's man of the year. That prediction did not come true, but the effectiveness of HAART was real. The death rate in the developed world fell by 80 percent by 1998.

Studies on **combination therapy** for HIV have shown that it can prevent HIV from mutating, as well as effectively slow down the replication of new HIV organisms. Combination therapy has also shown that it can increase the number of T4 cells, or helper cells in the blood, and that it allows patients to live longer. What has not been learned is how long the combination of drugs will remain effective.

Doctors tell patients about risks, benefits, and possible **side effects** of any drug therapy. Side effects are the unexpected and unwanted results that can happen by taking the drug. Side effects for anti-HIV drugs vary from person to person and drug to drug. Some increase the risk of heart disease, diabetes, and osteoporosis, a weakening of the bones to the point where they are likely to fracture. Side effects can make staying on the drug combination very difficult.

While no cure has been found for HIV, scientists have discovered a way to reduce infection. In 2011, it was announced that a dose of antiretroviral drugs taken orally every day by an uninfected person reduces that person's chance of becoming infected with HIV through heterosexual sex by 96 percent. This discovery was named the Breakthrough of the Year by *Science* magazine.

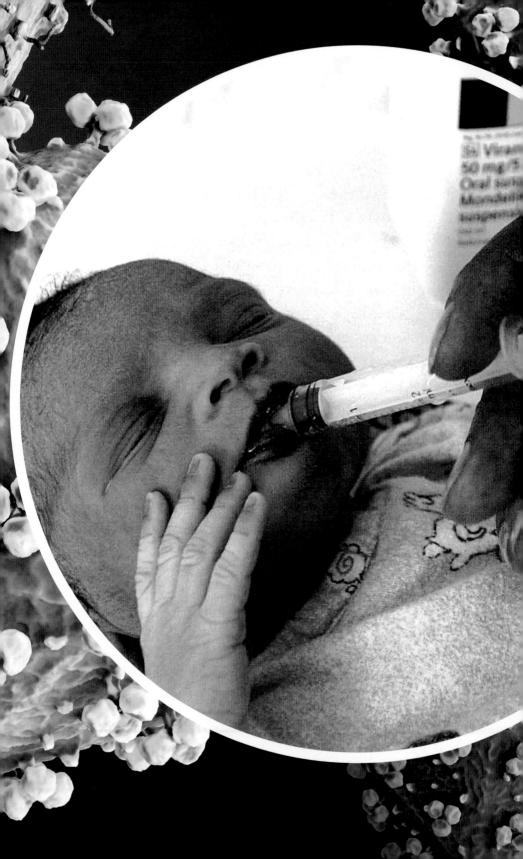

four The AIDS Battle Continues

The story of AIDS today is one of both success and failure. This is especially true when the worldwide status of the disease is considered. The AIDS virus has been a stubborn opponent. Even apparent victories against it have ended in defeat.

Doctors thought they had cured a three-year-old boy from Italy of the virus. His HIV-positive mother passed the virus on to him when he was born in 2009. Hours after his birth, doctors discovered he had a heavy **viral load**. Aggressive antiretroviral therapy began immediately. His HIV or viral load levels quickly dropped. At six months old they could not be detected. When antibodies to HIV left the boy's body, his mother gave doctors permission to stop the therapy.

However, the virus had been hiding in the memory cells deep within the boy's immune system. Doctors said that these memory cells are dormant or not active, so drugs used to get HIV out of someone's bloodstream can't get inside the cells to attack the virus. It was reported in October 2014, that two weeks after doctors

Doctors begin treating newborns who have a heavy viral load immediately.

43

ended treatment, the child had a relapse. That means that the virus had returned.

This is the second time a child thought to be cured relapsed. A four-year-old girl in Mississippi had lived free of HIV for two years before the virus returned.

HIV Still Striking

People are still contracting HIV. The CDC reports that there are close to fifty thousand cases of new infection in the United States every year. Rates of infection have fallen in some groups of people, including heterosexual women and those who inject drugs. However, this has been balanced by an increase in infections among gay and bisexual males.

Infection rates in this group fell from a high of about seventy-five thousand per year to a low of about eighteen thousand per year in the early 1990s. Since then, the infection rate among gay and bisexual males has reached thirty thousand per year. The greatest increase is among young African-American males ages thirteen to twenty-four.

Nations Affected

Infection rates are much higher in other countries, particularly in Africa south of the Sahara Desert. The World Health Organization (WHO) reports that 95 percent of all new infections occur in low- to middle-income countries. And in Sub-Saharan Africa, almost one out of every twenty adults is living with AIDS. The

AIDS orphans are cared for at a center that serves as a preschool in Malawi.

WHO also reported that there were 2.3 million new infections worldwide in 2012.

In countries where large numbers of adults have been killed by AIDS-related illnesses, many important roles in society such as educators, health care workers, and law enforcement officers are left vacant. Without enough people to fill these important roles, the quality of life in these countries declines rapidly.

A large number of adult deaths also leaves many children orphaned. If these children have no relatives to care for them, they are left to fend for themselves. Many have no way to feed themselves and have no access to basic medical care. Orphaned children are also at a greater risk of being infected with HIV themselves. Without parents or guardians, the children are more likely to be exposed to sexual abuse, thereby becoming infected with HIV.

Another challenge in these developing countries is getting antiretroviral therapy to people who need it. The number of people who are being treated has increased dramatically since 2003, but there are almost nineteen million people eligible for therapy who can't get the drugs.

Opportunistic Infections

In order for an HIV-infected person to develop AIDS, certain infections must also be present in addition to the HIV infection. These infections are called opportunistic infections. Opportunistic infections are illnesses that rarely cause disease or harm in persons with healthy immune systems. In persons with advanced HIV, however, opportunistic infections can develop into severe and sometimes fatal infections. They are called opportunistic infections because they use the opportunity of a weakened immune system to attack the host.

There are twenty-six opportunistic infections that the medical profession recognizes as an indication that a person's HIV infection has advanced into AIDS. A physician makes the diagnosis of AIDS after finding even one of the twenty-six present in an HIV patient.

When a person has tested positive for HIV but does not suffer any of the symptoms, the disease is in its asymptomatic stage. Asymptomatic literally means without symptoms. Even though there are no symptoms, the virus is reproducing around ten billion HIV germs a day.

AIDS Protection

Human Immunodeficiency Virus and Acquired Immunodeficiency Syndrome are not the same. We know that HIV causes AIDS, but people can have HIV and not have AIDS. It can take years for people with HIV to develop AIDS and to exhibit any symptoms.

The key is for people to be tested so treatment can start early. In a study released in 2014 it was found that early retroviral treatment reduces the risk of AIDS and HIV-related illnesses significantly. Early treatment can allow people with HIV to have a normal life expectancy, and it reduces the risk of transmitting HIV by 96 percent.

Not getting HIV is the best way to avoid getting AIDS. According to the Centers for Disease Control website:

"Consistent and correct use of the male latex condom reduces the risk of sexually transmitted disease (STD) and human immunodeficiency virus (HIV) transmission. However, condom use cannot provide absolute protection against any STD. The most reliable ways to avoid transmission of STDs are to abstain from sexual activity, or to be in a long-term mutually monogamous relationship with an uninfected partner. However, many infected persons may be unaware of their infection because STDs often are asymptomatic and unrecognized. Condoms can reduce the risk of being infected by HIV anywhere from 80 to 93 percent. And latex condoms fail at half the rate of other types of condoms."

The next stage of HIV infection is called the early symptomatic stage. This means that HIV is in the early stages of showing some symptoms. A person in the early symptomatic stage might experience any of the following symptoms of HIV infection:

- Frequent fevers
- Night sweats
- Rapid weight loss
- General fatigue
- Breathing difficulties
- Swollen lymph nodes
- Diarrhea that lasts longer than a week
- White spots or sores in the mouth and throat
- Pneumonia
- Memory loss
- Vision problems
- Depression
- Red, pink, purple, or brown blotches on or under the skin

In the late symptomatic stage, the immune system of an infected person begins to weaken. An infected person might experience more symptoms of the early symptomatic stage more frequently. In addition, new symptoms might occur such as:

- Shingles (a disease of the skin causing clusters of blisters)
- Persistent diarrhea

- Persistent fever
- Precancerous and cancerous growths
- Lung infections
- AIDS wasting syndrome

Wasting Away

AIDS wasting syndrome, often called "wasting" for short, can occur during any stage of HIV infection, but it is the most common symptom that indicates the HIV infection is getting worse. When an HIV positive person suffers from wasting, they lose more than 10 percent of their body weight. They may also experience persistent diarrhea, fever, and fatigue lasting more than a month. Wasting increases the risk of death in an HIV or AIDS patient as his or her body "wastes away."

Advanced HIV, or AIDS after a physician's diagnosis, can bring about other symptoms in addition to the symptoms of prior HIV stages. Symptoms of AIDS include the presence of certain cancers, mental disorders, and other opportunistic infections.

HIV/AIDS can be a very difficult subject for teenagers to discuss. However, there are very good reasons parents and children should talk about it. The biggest one is that many teenagers get infections that don't show up until they are young adults. The number of teens becoming infected has been increasing. Less than 2 percent of teens consider HIV as a reason to not have sex.

Glimmers of Hope

When Magic Johnson revealed that he was HIV positive in 1991, it made more people realize that they could get the virus. Knowing this, many more heterosexual people went for testing.

Testing is very important. Many people infected with HIV don't know they have it. According to the CDC, of the estimated 1,178,350 people in the United States living with HIV, about 240,000 are unaware of their infection. An estimated 21.4 percent of the half million African Americans who are infected don't know they have the virus.

A person can be infected, and infect others, even if there are no symptoms of any illness. HIV can live in a person's body for years without causing any symptoms. AIDS develops at the end of a long process of HIV infection. The term AIDS is a diagnosis used to describe people suffering from the advanced stages of HIV infection.

The best defense against HIV is saying no to people who want you to engage in high-risk behavior.

Many people do not immediately develop symptoms of illness with HIV. Other people develop a flu-like sickness within two months of becoming HIV infected. In most cases, the symptoms will disappear shortly after appearing, so the infected person might never guess that the sickness was due to HIV infection.

The CDC has started programs to increase AIDS testing, and President Barack Obama has expanded support for increasing treatment of HIV patients and for testing. It has been found that people engaging in high-risk behavior are most successful at convincing other people to get tested. There are programs that pay small amounts to someone who refers another person for testing. Many more people who are HIV positive are found that way than in traditional programs.

In order for a doctor to diagnose a patient with HIV or AIDS, the patient must take medical blood tests. Since HIV-infected people often lack symptoms for several years, a person must examine their past and present activities when considering the possibility of having HIV or AIDS. A person should take HIV blood tests or tell someone to take HIV blood tests if he or she has:

- had unprotected sex with an infected partner,
- had unprotected sex with someone whom they didn't know very well,
- have more than one sexual partner,
- used and shared needles with others, or
- received tattoos or piercings from a used, unclean needle.

If a person is doing or has done any of these activities, it's a good idea for that person to speak with a doctor about taking an HIV test. Taking the test lets infected people know if they need medical attention. People who have HIV and continue to lead a lifestyle that involves HIV infection risks will spread HIV to others.

A good time to take an HIV test is anywhere from three to six months after realizing that you have put yourself at risk for HIV infection. People who know that they have put themselves at risk should stop all HIV-risk activities and get tested.

There are steps that you can take that will help you to avoid becoming infected with HIV.

- Avoid unprotected sexual contact.
- Do not share hypodermic needles.
- Use only specially cleaned needles for tattoos or piercings.

Saying No to High-Risk Behavior

Throughout life, we are faced many times with decisions that can change us forever. By saying, "yes" to any HIV high-risk activity, you can almost guarantee that your life will never be the same. Just as you wouldn't wish sickness on anyone that you love, you should love yourself enough to avoid any sickness, if possible.

Saying "no" to sex or drug use can be very difficult for some—but avoidance of these two behaviors is protection against disease. There are many things that

Marrow transplants rid Timothy Brown of HIV and leukemia.

The Man Who Was Cured

Only one person has ever been cured of AIDS, but it
came with a high cost. Timothy Brown is a gay man
who was found to be HIV positive in 1995. Eleven
years later, he was diagnosed with leukemia.
Chemotherapy failed, so his last option was
for someone to donate bone marrow for a
stem-cell transplant.

His doctor, Gero Hütter, knew that some people with a natural genetic mutation are resistant to the virus. HIV attaches itself to cells with a receptor called CD4. A receptor sits on the outside of a cell, and it sends messages into the cell. CD4 is needed for our immune systems to work. People with the genetic mutation don't have a protein called CCR5. This is also a receptor and it works with CD4. It allows HIV to enter a cell. So Hütter searched worldwide for a donor with this mutation who was also an immune system match for Brown. Hütter wanted to cure Brown of both HIV and leukemia. One donor was found.

Two transplants were needed, and Brown was eventually cured of both illnesses. However, the cure is not for everyone. Bone marrow transplants from unrelated donors are often fatal. They cost $250,000 and are a good risk only for someone who will otherwise die. Also, Brown suffered neurological damage—his speech is affected—from his treatment.

To his credit, he has allowed himself to be tested many times. Scientists have made discoveries from those tests that have put them on a path that could lead to a cure for AIDS.

you can say in addition to "No thanks" that should be accepted as your reasons for not doing something harmful. Your friends, boyfriend or girlfriend, or family members should accept any of your reasons. You can respond "no" to pressure about sex or drugs by saying things such as:

- I am not ready, and since it is my body, I will tell you when I am ready.
- Sex doesn't interest me.
- I am very sure. My answer is no, but thanks.
- I care about you, but I don't want to do it. Let's do something else.
- To me, sex outside of marriage is wrong.
- Drugs don't interest me.
- I am taking care of my body, and drugs will harm my body.
- I will not break the law, and drugs are illegal.

There is still no cure for AIDS, and treatments can cost tens of thousands of dollars each year, be painful, and fail—so people die. There have been a few advances in medical research, but any possible cure may be decades away. Anyone engaged in high-risk behaviors should take all known precautions to keep from contracting the disease.

Seeking Answers

Doctors know that getting rid of CCR5 receptors in cells makes it impossible for HIV to get started. They are working on proteins that cut out the genetic code that produces the CCR5 receptors. This creates a cell that resists HIV.

Researchers are also trying to wake up the dormant virus in people — the kind of virus that infected the children who were thought to be HIV free. If they can do that, they can get rid of HIV. There are several substances that can wake up a dormant virus, but so far they have proved toxic to people. Tests on compounds conducted by Johns Hopkins University failed when they were used on white blood cells taken from people with HIV.

Most money spent on AIDS research has been used to care for people with the disease. The National Institute of Health's National Institute of Allergy and Infectious Diseases spent only 3 percent of its AIDS research budget on finding a cure in 2009. Also, the world's economy has suffered since 2008, leaving less money both for AIDS research and funding treatment for the poor. This is a growing problem with more people being infected each year than there are patients starting treatment.

In 2012, President Obama announced the National Institutes of Health would move $100 million in research funds into programs to find a cure for AIDS. With other countries also pledging support for medical research, the goal of an AIDS-free generation eventually might be reached.

Glossary

Acquired Immunodeficiency Syndrome (AIDS)
A disease caused by infection with HIV.

antibody A natural substance made by B cells to fight a specific infection.

B Cell A type of white blood cell that produces antibodies.

combination therapy Treatment that uses more than one kind of drug to treat a disease or infection.

germ A small organism that can cause disease and infection.

hemophilia A condition where a person, called a hemophiliac, cannot stop bleeding from a cut or wound.

Human Immunodeficiency Virus (HIV) An infectious virus that causes the eventual development of the disease AIDS.

immune system The body's defense system against illness, disease, and infection.

Kaposi's sarcoma A rare cancer that is most likely caused by a virus.

lesion A scratch, bump, wound, or other abnormality in the tissue of the body.

lymphadenopathy A disease affecting the lymph nodes.

lymph node Areas where immune reactions occur. They are found in the neck, armpit, groin, and internal body.

plasma The watery part of blood that contains blood cells.

protease inhibitor A drug that prevents the enzyme protease from working. HIV uses protease to multiply.

side effect Any unwanted result of taking a drug or treatment.

T cell Cells of the immune system.

transmission The spread of a disease or infection.

vaccine A medicine that causes an immune response.

viral load The amount of virus in a tested sample of blood or body fluid.

virus A germ that needs a living organism in order to to survive and multiply.

white blood cells Cells of the immune system that protect the body from harmful organisms and substances.

For More Information

Websites

How Stuff Works Infectious Diseases

health.howstuffworks.com/diseases-conditions/
infectious

This website provides background on infectious diseases
and the epidemics they have caused.

National Geographic Health and Human Body

science.nationalgeographic.com/science/health-and-
human-body

Get the latest information on diseases and how the
body works.

World Health Organization Infectious Diseases

www.who.int/topics/infectious_diseases/en

Learn more about the organization created to monitor
and fight disease worldwide. Get facts and the latest
information on infectious diseases, including HIV/AIDS.

Organizations

AIDS Treatment Information Service (ATIS)
PO Box 6303
Rockville, MD 20849-6303
800-HIV-0440 (800-448-0440)

Interested in learning more about HIV and AIDS?
Check out these websites and organizations.

800-822-7422 (Project Inform)
TTY: 888-480-3739 / International: 301-519-0459
www.hivatis.org

Canadian AIDS Society
130 Albert Street, Suite 900
Ottawa, Canada K1P 5G4
613-230-3580
www.cdnaids.ca

Centers for Disease Control (CDC)
1600 Clifton Road
Atlanta, GA 30333
404-639-3534 / 800-311-3435

CDC National AIDS Hotline
800-342-AIDS (2437)
Spanish: 800-344-SIDA (7432) / Deaf: 800-243-7889
www.cdc.gov

National Minority AIDS Council
300 I Street NW, Suite 400
Washington, DC 20002
202-544-1076
www.nmac.org

For Further Reading

Books

Farrell, Jeanette. *Invisible Enemies: Stories of Infectious Disease*. 2nd ed. New York: Farrar, Straus and Giroux, 2005.

Gardy, Jennifer. *It's Catching: The Infectious World of Germs and Microbes*. Toronto, Ontario: Owlkids Books, 2014.

Pepin, Jacques. *The Origin of AIDS*. Cambridge, England: Cambridge University Press, 2011.

Websites

Aids.gov. A Timeline of AIDS. www.aids.gov/hiv-aids-basics/hiv-aids-101/aids-timeline

Hobbes, Michael. *New Republic*. Why Did AIDS Ravage the U.S. More Than Any Other Developed Country? www.newrepublic.com/article/117691/aids-hit-united-states-harder-other-developed-countries-why

Keim, Brandon. *National Geographic*. Early Spread of AIDS Traced to Congo's Expanding Transportation Network. news.nationalgeographic.com/news/2014/10/141002-hiv-virus-spread-africa-health

McNeil, Donald G. *New York Times*. Chimp to Man to History Books: The Path of AIDS. www.nytimes.com/2011/10/18/health/18aids.html?pagewanted=all&_r=0

Index

Index